More to explore

On some of the pages in this book, you will find coloured buttons with symbols on them. There are four different colours, and each belongs to a different topic. Choose a topic, follow its coloured buttons through the book, and you'll make some interesting discoveries of your own.

For example, on page 6 you'll find an orange button, like this, next to the picture of Earth. The orange buttons are about forms of life.

Page 22

Life

There is a page number in the button. Turn to that page (page 22) to find an orange button next to another example of life on Earth. Follow all the steps through the book, and at the end of your journey you'll find out how the steps are linked and discover even more information about this topic.

Science

Environment

People

The other topics in this book are science, environment and people. Follow the steps and see what you can discover!

4

Our planet, our home

What do people mean when they talk about our planet? Well, they mean the huge ball of rock and other material that we all live on. Our planet – Earth – is the only one we know of that is home to living things.

Water covers two-thirds of Earth's surface. Most of this water is salty water, held in the oceans.

Boats allow people to cross the oceans.

Earth, like all planets, is shaped like a ball.

This is the Atlantic Ocean, close to Central and South America.

Earth has been photographed by satellites in space. This photo shows blue oceans, green land and yellow-brown mountains. From space, all clouds look white.

Earth, seen from space

THE BATTLE OF CHAERONEA

Some Greeks saw **Phillip** and the Macedonians as a menace; others thought he might be able to **unite** Greece as a country at last. Finally, the years of minor battles and disagreements came to a head, and a great battle was fought outside the town of **Chaeronea**, in the middle of Greece. The Macedonian forces were too powerful for the **Athenians**, even with the help of the Thebans, and **Phillip** easily won. All the Greek city-states (except Sparta) agreed to work together and become the **League of Corinth**, loyal to **Phillip**. **Phillip** agreed to keep the peace between the city-states. Greece was (almost) **united** at last.

THE BATTLE OF CHAERONEA

PHILLIP II WAS <u>ASSASSINATED</u> AT HIS DAUGHTER'S WEDDING. HE WAS STABBED BY ONE OF HIS OWN BODYGUARDS.

AARGH!

AARGH!

WAIT, WHAT?
TO PRONOUNCE THESE WORDS, SAY:

MACEDONIA = MASS-EH-DOH-NEE-AH

CHAERONEA = KER-U-NEE-U

19

ALEXANDER THE GREAT

LET'S GO CONQUER EVERYTHING!

Greece now had a new ruler: Phillip's son, Alexander. Alexander was only 20, but he had already seen many battles and had fought at Chaeronea at only 18 years old. Alexander wasted no time becoming a mighty ruler, and he set off to fight just about anyone who stood in his way.

WOO HOO! I'M YOUNG, I'M HEALTHY, I'M A GOOD-LOOKING GUY, AND I'M KING OF, WELL, JUST ABOUT ANYTHING I WANT! I'VE GOT A GREAT COLLECTION OF COUNTRIES IN MY CONTROL NOW. I'M THE RULER OF GREECE, THE KING OF PERSIA, AND I'VE TAKEN OVER EGYPT AND BUILT A MASSIVE CITY CALLED ALEXANDRIA! WHY NOT, RIGHT? I'VE JUST ADDED A BIT OF INDIA TO MY COLLECTION... WHERE NEXT?

In theory, the Greek empire is growing now, and Alexander wants to take over the whole world... So how did it all disappear?

The Empire of
**Alexander
the Great**
and his conquest course
from Greece to India
to Babylon (334-323 B.C.)

MURDER MYSTERY?

After surviving battle after battle, Alexander suddenly died. No-one is really sure how he died. Some people think he was poisoned, while others think he got a disease such as **TYPHOID FEVER** or **MALARIA**. However good things might have seemed for the Greek empire, they were going to change a lot after Alexander was gone...

With an effort he looked at them as they passed

WHILE ALEXANDER LAY DYING, HIS SOLDIERS WERE ALLOWED TO PASS BY HIM TO LOOK AT HIM ONE LAST TIME.

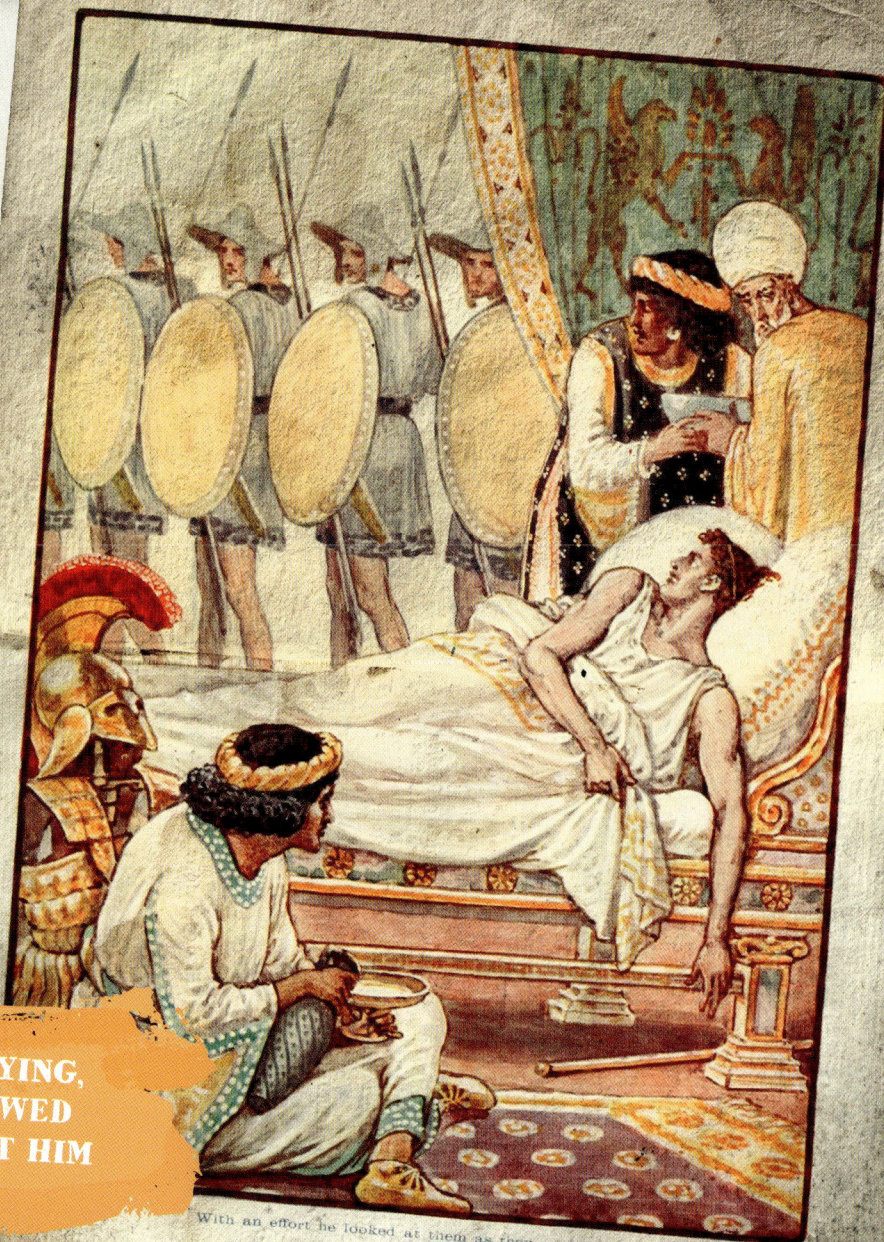

HELLENISTIC GREECE

323 BC–31 BC

Alexander died without leaving an **HEIR**, and so his enormous empire was divided up among his **GENERALS**. Back in Greece, the city-states were able to have a little more freedom, although they were still under Macedonia's control.

> JUST BECAUSE I, PTOLEMY I SOTER, AM KING OF EGYPT NOW, I CAN'T SEE ANY REASON WHY I SHOULD BECOME EGYPTIAN AT ALL! I'M NOT LEARNING THE LANGUAGE AND I'LL JUST STAY HERE IN ALEXANDRIA. ALEXANDRIA IS THE MOST GREEK PLACE IN THE WORLD. WHAT DO YOU MEAN, IT'S NOT IN GREECE? THAT DOESN'T MATTER - IT'S STILL VERY GREEK, ISN'T IT? AND THAT'S WHAT MATTERS.

PTOLEMY I SOTER TOOK OVER EGYPT AS PHARAOH AFTER ALEXANDER THE GREAT DIED.

Even though we call this time the Hellenistic age (Hellas means Greece and Hellenic means Greek), there wasn't really a united Greek empire at all. Greece itself had been taken over by the Antigonids of Macedonia. Once again, the Greek peoples were split into states, cities and neighbouring empires. Could they ever come together, or would the Greek empire never fulfil its potential?

CAN THEY ALL STOP FIGHTING LONG ENOUGH TO SAVE THEMSELVES?

WISHING TO BE FRIENDS IS QUICK WORK, BUT FRIENDSHIP IS A SLOW RIPENING FRUIT.

...ERM, WHAT?

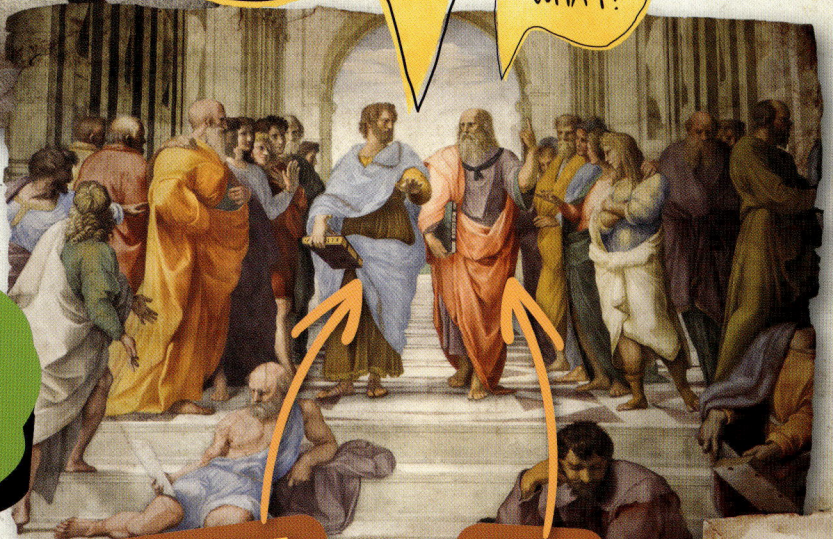

ARISTOTLE

PLATO

WAIT, WHAT?
TO PRONOUNCE THESE WORDS, SAY:

PTOLEMY = TOLL-U-MEE
HELLENISTIC = HELL-EN-ISS-TIK
ANTIGONIDS = ANN-TIG-U-NIDS

23

THE ROMAN EMPIRE

The Roman Empire

Mare Germanicum

Britannia

Belgica

Germania Superior

Lugdunensis

Oceanus Atlanticus

Noricum

Aquitania

Raetia

Pannonia

Narbonensis

Dacia

Italia

Dalmatia

Moesia

Pontus Euxinus

Tarraconensis

Corsica

Roma

Macedonia

Thracia

Lusitania

Sardinia

Epirus

Bithynia et Pontus

Armenia

Baetica

Asia

Galatia

Cappadocia

Sicilia

Lycia

Cilicia

Achaia

Mauretania

Africa

Mare Internum

Syria

Assyria

Cyprus

Mesopotamia

Iudaea

Cyrenaica

Arabia Petraea

Aegyptus

THE AREA IN RED SHOWS THE AREAS CONTROLLED BY THE ROMANS IN AD 117.

Let's go forward a few hundred years. The Greeks had been doing their usual thing: splitting up, having wars, forming new alliances, splitting up... and so on. But all the while, the Roman Empire had been creeping across Europe, and in 146 BC it reached Corinth. The Roman Empire was an enormous, unstoppable force, and it smashed the Greeks at the Battle of Corinth. This was the beginning of Roman rule in Greece.

Weather happens in the air that surrounds Earth.

The highest point of a mountain is called the peak, or summit. ......

Lightning may strike in stormy weather. ......

Low valleys lie between mountains.

The land is where Earth's surface sticks out above the oceans. Land can be flat, hilly or mountainous. Most land is covered with soil and has grass or other plants growing on it.

butterflies

African elephants

People live in different countries in different parts of the world. Earth is home to more than 6 billion people.

Elephants are the biggest land animals. ......

Animals, plants, fungi, bacteria and all sorts of other living things share our planet. Some live on land and others live in the oceans.

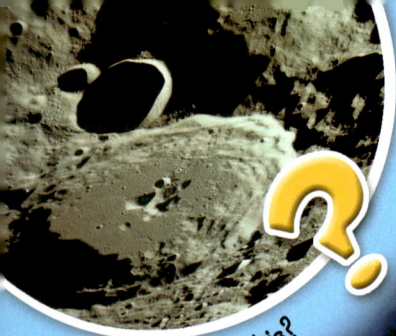

What is this?

1

2

Page 22

Earth in space

Earth is one of billions of objects in space. Our planet circles around the Sun, and the Moon circles around our planet. The Sun is actually a star, one of millions in our galaxy. Our galaxy is called the Milky Way. There are many millions of galaxies in space.

> SULLA HERE, ROMAN GENERAL. I'M ON MY WAY BACK TO ROME AFTER A VISIT TO THAT LITTLE PROVINCE WE CALL GREECE. KING MITHRIDATES PUT UP A BIT OF A REBELLION, SO WE HAD TO SQUASH THAT, AND WE TOOK CONTROL OF ATHENS WHILE WE WERE THERE! I'VE DONE EVER SO WELL, I'VE GOT 40,000 MEN WITH ME NOW AND LOTS AND LOTS OF <u>PLUNDER</u>. I'LL BE A HERO BACK HOME...

PAX ROMANA

The Roman Empire entered a long period of peace. This is known as the **Pax Romana**. The Romans settled in Greece, bringing their own traditions and beliefs with them. Religions such as **Judaism** and **Christianity** started to mix with the beliefs in the old gods of ancient Greece. Slowly, during the **Pax Romana**, the time of the great philosophers and thinkers came to an end as Greek culture mixed with that of the Romans. The Romans liked Greek culture. Things such as languages (Greek and Latin) and culture became blended until a new era had begun. The Greco-Roman period was on its way, and the old ways of Zeus and Athena were forgotten...

WAIT, WHAT?
TO PRONOUNCE THESE WORDS, SAY:

SULLA = SULL-AH
MITHRIDATES = MITH-RID-AY-TEEZ

25

RISE AND FALL AND RISE AND FALL...

CULTURE, COUNTRY OR CIVILISATION?

ALEXANDRIA, EGYPT

AHH, ALEXANDRIA, CENTRE OF GREEK CULTURE...

ERM, AREN'T WE IN EGYPT?

It's hard to stick a pin in a timeline and say: that's the moment ancient Greece ended. This is partly because ancient Greece was never a country or a place; it was a set of ideas, politics, traditions and values. Athenians, Spartans, Thebans, Corinthians, Macedonians and even Egyptian pharaohs all thought of themselves as being Greek, no matter where they were from. Even the mighty Roman Empire couldn't get rid of this completely. It is easy to conquer territory, but much harder to conquer ideas.

26

So, whatever happened to the ancient Greeks? The answer lies in asking when the ideas of this civilisation died out. So much of what made the Greeks unique is part of our modern culture today. Historians call this a foundation culture. This means a culture that continues to affect the countries and civilisations that come after it, even for thousands of years.

The ancient Greeks affected our language, books, mathematics, art, schools, ideas, politics, drama, science and medicine. If we say that these were the things that made them who they were, can we say they really went anywhere at all?

WHAT REMAINS OF THE ANCIENTS?

THE GREEKS SHALL INHERIT THE WORLD

Greece today is a modern place, with bustling cities and a thriving culture all of its own. But if you travel to modern-day Athens, you can trek up the to the Acropolis and take a selfie at the Parthenon. Greece may not feel the same, but its history is all around us in the present day. Let's take a look at how this civilisation affects us now...

THE OLYMPICS

DO YOU WATCH THE OLYMPICS? WHEN YOU DO, YOU ARE WATCHING THE MODERN VERSION OF THE ANCIENT GAMES, INVENTED BY THE ANCIENT GREEKS.

DEMOCRACY

If you can go with a grown-up to a **POLLING STATION**, or if you can vote on things in your school or class, you are taking part in democracy – the modern version of Cleisthenes's idea of demokratia. Each person gets one vote, and the idea or person with the most votes wins.

Over the years, women and other groups have had to fight for their right to vote – it's become a very special idea. Around the world, not everyone has the vote – but many people still campaign to have their say.

THERE ARE LOTS OF GREEK WORDS THAT HAVE STAYED IN OUR LANGUAGE FOR THOUSANDS OF YEARS. THERE ARE OVER 150,000 WORDS IN MODERN ENGLISH THAT COME FROM ANCIENT GREEK WORDS.

WORDS

SUFFRAGETTES LIKE ME, GRACE CHAPPELOW, FOUGHT TO WIN THE RIGHT TO VOTE. VOTING AND DEMOCRACY IS VERY IMPORTANT AND EVERYONE SHOULD HAVE A SAY IN HOW THEIR COUNTRY IS RUN.

ACROBAT, CEMETERY, DINOSAUR, EUROPE, GALAXY, MUSIC, PANIC, PHOBIA, PLANET, TELESCOPE…

VOTES FOR WOMEN

VOTES FOR WOMEN

SOME CLEVER MATHS

THEATRE

CAN SUCH A MAN, SO DESPERATE, STILL BOAST HE CAN SAVE HIS LIFE FROM THE FLASHING BOLTS OF GOD?

$68 + 452 + 725 + 4361 + (762 + 250) + (750 \times 46) +$
$462 + 2800 + 52 \div$
$(48000 + 652) +$
$95 + 65$

IT'S A DOODLE, ARISTOTLE!

GLOSSARY

ALLIANCES
agreements or pacts where two countries promise to work together

ARCHITECTS
people who design structures

ARMY
a group of soldiers that fight on land

ARTEFACTS
objects made by humans in history

ASSASSINATED
killed for reasons to do with power or religion

CITY-STATES
cities that are surrounded by land, in which everything belongs to one state

CONVULSIONS
sudden movements made by the body that the person cannot stop

CULTURE
the way of life and traditions of a group of people

EMPIRE
a group of countries or states that are owned by one ruler or country

ERA
a period of time

EXPANDING
getting bigger

GENERALS
commanders of an army, or very important officers who are high up in the army

HEIR
someone who will get the objects, money and titles of a person who dies

HOPLITES
heavily armoured soldiers of ancient Greece who would fight on foot

ICONIC
when something is well-known and a symbol of a place or time

IMMORTAL
will live forever

IMPORT
to bring food or objects into a country from abroad

MALARIA
a fever spread by mosquitoes in tropical and subtropical places

NAVY
the part of the armed services that fights at sea, made up of sailors and boats

OATH
a serious, important promise

PHILOSOPHY
learning and studying life, knowledge and lots of important human topics

PLUNDER
objects, money and other things that have been obtained illegally

POLITICIANS
people involved with politics and how the country is run

POLLING STATION
a place where people vote during an election

RECONSTRUCT
build again, using clues from before

SIEGE
an attack where the army surrounds a town or building and stops anything going in or out

TOGAS
pieces of clothing worn in ancient times, which were usually loose and covered the whole body

TRUCE
an agreement made between enemies or opponents to stop fighting

TYPHOID FEVER
a type of disease which caused problems such as spots, fever and diarrhoea

UNITED
joined or working together

INDEX

PHOTO CREDITS

All images are courtesy of Shutterstock.com, unless otherwise specified. With thanks to Getty Images, Thinkstock Photo and iStockphoto. Front Cover – Anastasios71, Naty_Lee, studioworkstock, Dean Drobot, anyaivanova, pupahava. 4&5 – cge2010, MicroOne, Eroshka, Linda Bucklin. 6&7 – Eugene Ga, Anastasios71, DM7, Free Wind 2014, The Story of Greece: Told to boys and girls by Macgregor, Mary, Noemi D, Tymonko Galyna, Good_Stock, delcarmat. 8&9 – Lukasz Soltan, Renata Sedmakova, Vasileios Karafillidis, anyaivanova, Lola Pankratova. 10&11 – Maxim Maksutov, nikolpetr, GaudiLab. 12&13 – Jastrow, douglasmack. 14&15 – milosk50, Kizel Cotiw-an, Tilemahos Efthimiadis, Wayback Machine. 16&17 – Digital Storm, Elenarts, Mr. Rashad, Arizzona Design. 18&19 – Edmund Ollier Publication date 1882, Ellis, Edward Sylvester. 20&21 – Brigida Soriano, Peter Hermes Furian, Walter Crane. 22&23 – Fotokvadrat, serato. 24&25 – delcarmat, Peter Hermes Furian. 26&27 – AlexMorozov1204, Voropaev Vasiliy, Chelmsford Museum, Eroshka, Ollyy, Pit Stock. 28&29 – AlexMorozov1204, Voropaev Vasiliy, Chelmsford Museum, Eroshka, Ollyy, Pit Stock. Paper – ZaZa Studio, Monica Butnaru, Ints Vikmanis, ZaZa Studio, Anton Watman. Speech Bubbles – Nataleana. Caption banner – Olga_C

3

6

Earth moves around the Sun in an oval-shaped path called an orbit. There are seven other planets orbiting our Sun too. Scientists use satellites like the one below to help them investigate the wonders of space. They take photographs and gather other information. Scientists are still looking for signs of life on other planets.

5

4

Page 27

This photograph shows pits, called craters, on the surface of the Moon.

Earth, Sun and Moon

The Sun and Moon affect many things that happen on Earth. For example, the Sun gives us light and warmth, which most living things need to survive. The Moon affects the oceans, causing tides.

Sun

Here it is night-time.

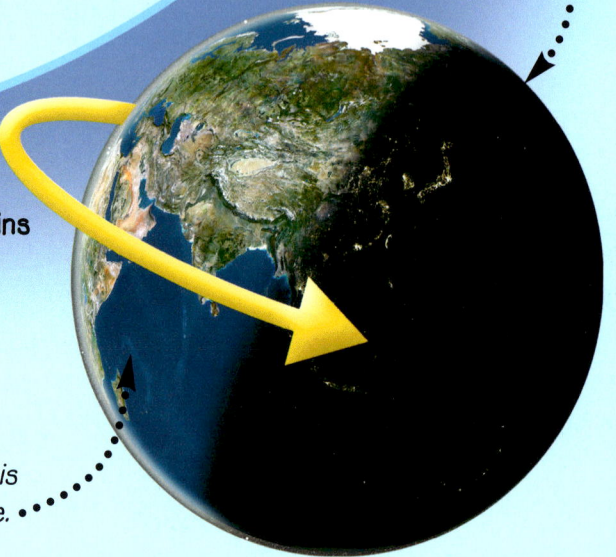

Earth spins round and round as it orbits the Sun. It takes 24 hours, or one day, to complete each turn. Parts of Earth facing the Sun receive daylight. In parts that are facing away, it is night.

Earth spins on a tilt.

Here it is daytime.

Plants have leaves to help catch sunlight.

Sunlight is very important for life on Earth. Plants need sunlight to grow, and they provide us and many animals with food. The Sun also warms our planet. It drives the winds, rain and other types of weather too.

Children pick vegetables in Hawaii, USA.

Sunrise lights
up the sky.

The Sun rises in the morning, when our part of Earth is moving into daylight. It sets as we move into night. The Sun is far away in space, but we can see it in the sky because it is so huge. The Sun is 109 times wider than Earth!

Cold winter weather
can bring snow and ice.

Seasons happen because Earth orbits the Sun once every year. When it is summer, our part of Earth is tilted towards the Sun during daytime, so we receive more of its heat and light. In winter we get less sunlight as our part of Earth tilts slightly away.

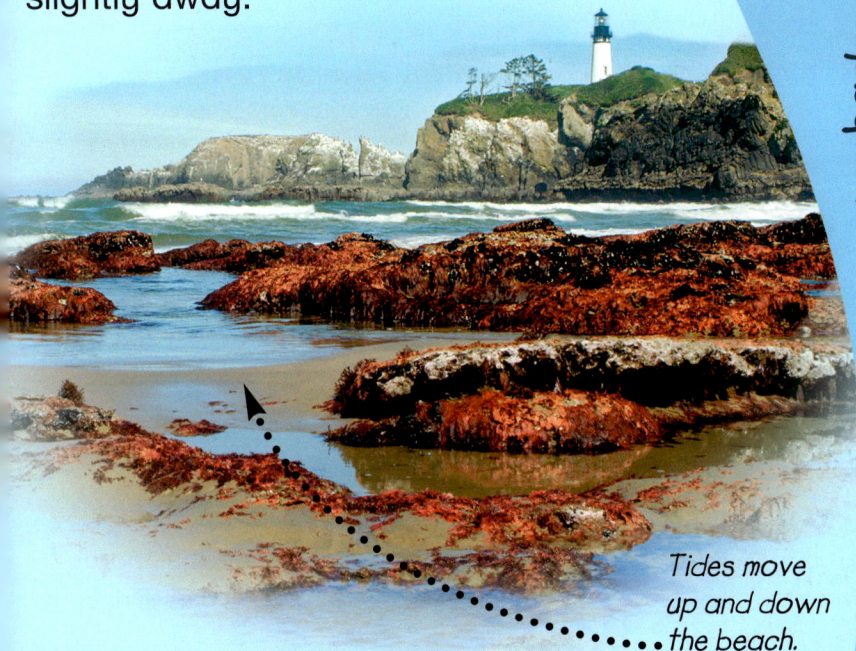

Like Earth,
the Moon is
lit by the Sun.

Earth's shadow often covers part of the Moon, so it looks like a crescent.

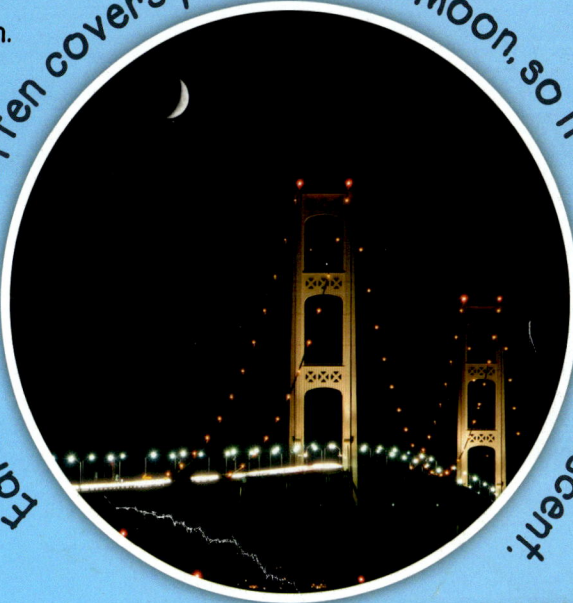

In an eclipse
the Moon
blocks out
the Sun.

Tides move
up and down
the beach.

A solar eclipse is when the Moon passes right between Earth and the Sun. The Moon is much smaller than the Sun, but it looks the same size because it is closer to us.

Tides in the ocean are caused by the Moon. As the Moon moves around Earth, it pulls the water on Earth's surface towards it. Twice every day, the sea moves away from the shore and back in again.

What is this?

1 red-hot lava   2 crater filled with magma   3 smoke and ash

2

1

Page 18

Volcanic eruption!

There are few natural sights as spectacular as a volcanic eruption. Smoke, ash and scorching lava pour out of the Earth, causing chaos and destruction. People living near active volcanoes must be ready to escape at any time.

3

Page 19

5

The people of this farming village are being evacuated to safety, as rivers of red-hot lava pour towards their homes. When a volcano erupts, lava can burn down houses. Ash fills the air and covers buildings and land. Eruptions can go on for days, weeks or even years. Their effects often spread for many kilometres around.

Page 15

4

6

This is a close-up view of lava with a cooled, hardened crust on top.

Inside Earth

Earth is made up of different layers. On the outside is the crust, where we live. Inside it is much hotter, sometimes so hot that the rocks are liquid. The sizzling centre of Earth is called the core.

Earth's crust is between 5 and 50 kilometres thick. It is made up of sections called plates, which float on the mantle beneath.

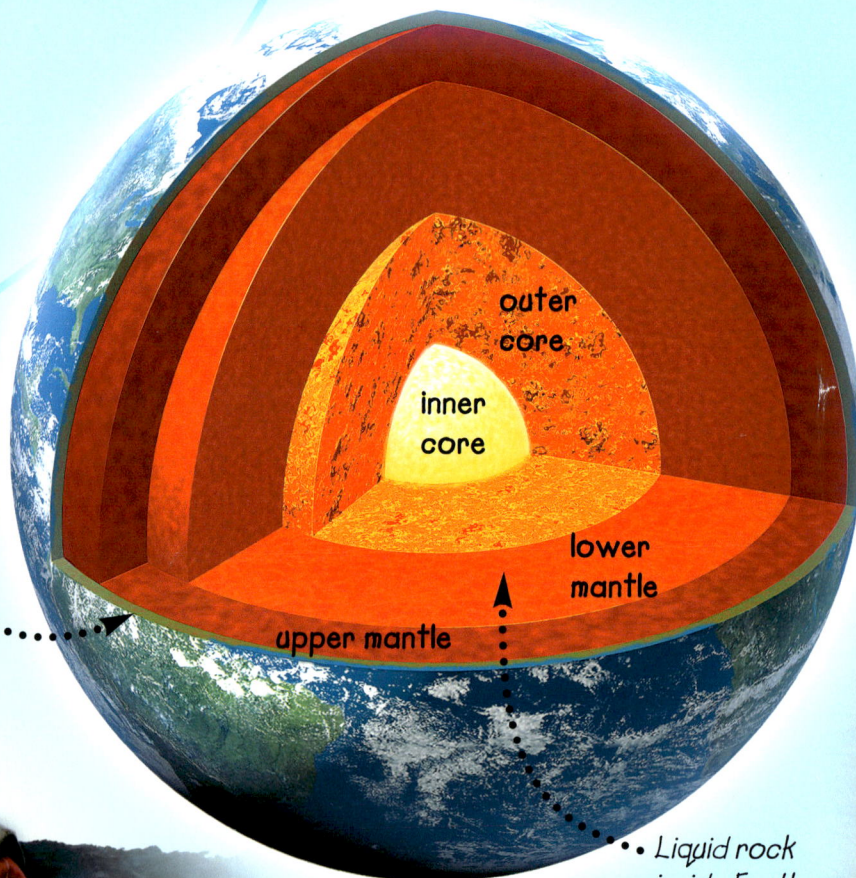

The temperature of lava ranges from 700 to 1,300°C.

Land and oceans lie on Earth's crust.

outer core

inner core

lower mantle

upper mantle

Liquid rock inside Earth is called magma.

Lava is liquid rock that has burst through Earth's crust, usually from a volcano. When lava cools, it hardens and becomes solid. The rock it forms is called igneous rock. There are two other main types of rock: sedimentary and metamorphic.

A volcanologist studies lava from a volcano.

An earthquake takes place when two plates in Earth's crust jerk suddenly against each other. This causes the ground to shake.

Earthquakes happen along fault lines like this, where two plates meet.

This is the San Andreas fault in California, USA.

Valuable stones and metals are hidden in Earth's crust. In some places people dig holes, called mines, to find them.

Gold is a precious metal found in some rock.

This crown is made of gold and jewels.

The jewels are stones dug from Earth's crust.

Fossil fuels, such as oil and coal, also come from Earth's crust. They lie in sedimentary rocks – rocks made from mud, sand or other sediments that were buried in the past.

An oil rig drills for oil in rock under the ocean.

Mountain adventure

Earth has areas of land and sea, and the land has many forms. Mountains are huge, steep-sided rock masses that rise up from Earth's crust. They are found where plates in the crust have crashed together, pushing up giant folds of rock. The tops of mountains are the highest places on our planet.

Page 30

What is this?

?

1. Loose snow falls in an avalanche.

2. valley made by a glacier, or river of ice

3. distant mountain peaks

? This is a magnified snowflake. All snowflakes have six points and every one is slightly different.

Page 23

These climbers are on a slope in the Himalayas – the highest mountain range on Earth. Up here it is cold and windy and the air is thin, making it difficult to breathe. Mountaineers take special equipment and clothing to help them survive.

Page 19

4 Mountain peaks are often above cloud level.

5 Climbers use maps and satellite devices to find their way.

6 An oxygen tank and mask help climbers to breathe.

On the map

Maps are pictures that mark out places on Earth's surface. On world maps like this one we can see both land and sea. Maps can give us lots of information, including how high the land is and where different countries and cities are found.

Countries are marked on some maps by lines called borders. Country borders are decided by people. There are 195 countries in the world.

Islands are areas of land that are surrounded by water. The photograph below shows an island in French Polynesia.

On a map, French Polynesia is here. It lies in the Pacific Ocean.

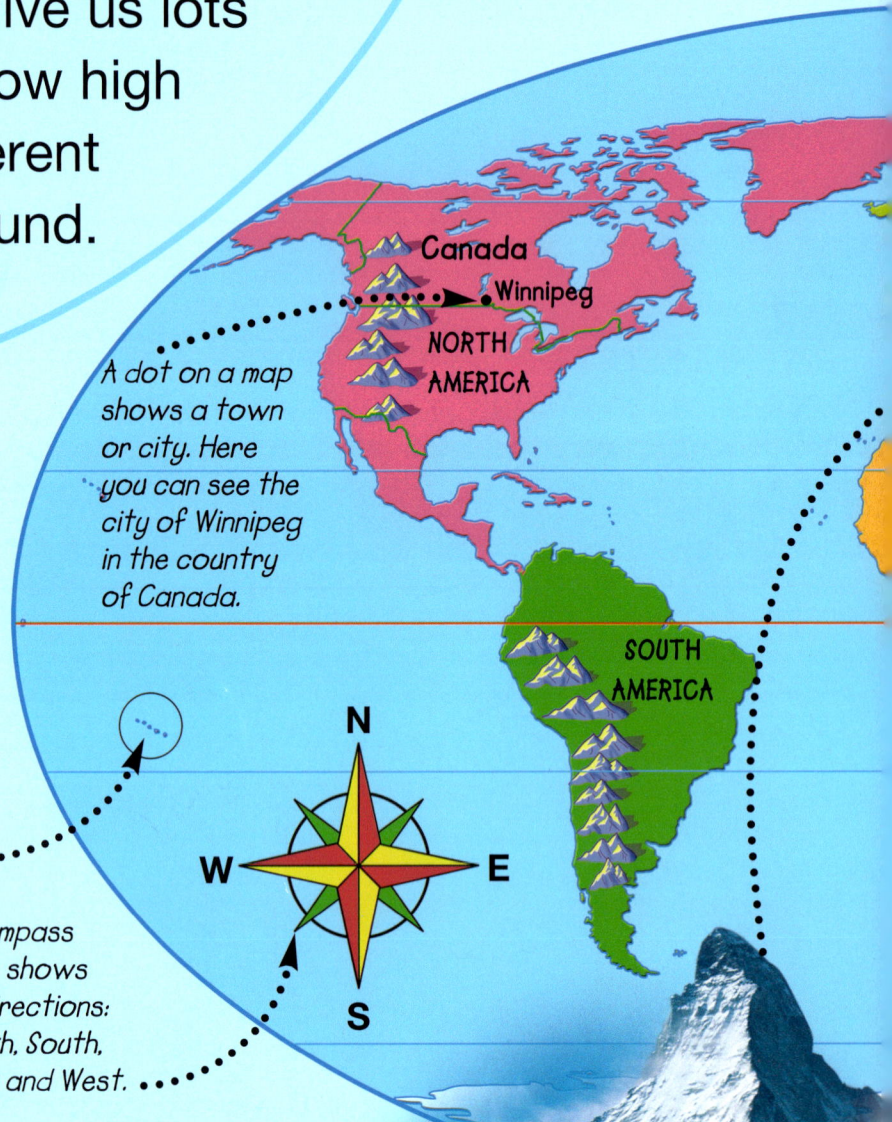

A dot on a map shows a town or city. Here you can see the city of Winnipeg in the country of Canada.

A compass rose shows us directions: North, South, East and West.

Canada
Winnipeg
NORTH AMERICA
SOUTH AMERICA
N S E W

Alps

Mountain ranges are drawn as symbols on this map. The tallest are the Himalayas in Asia. This skier is in the Alps, a mountain range in Europe.

Continents are the main land masses on Earth. Here the seven continents are shown in different colours. Asia is the largest continent in the world and has more people than any other continent.

A globe shows the world as it really is – ball-shaped rather than flat, like maps. Most globes show each country in a different colour. They also show the poles and the Equator, an imaginary line around the middle of Earth.

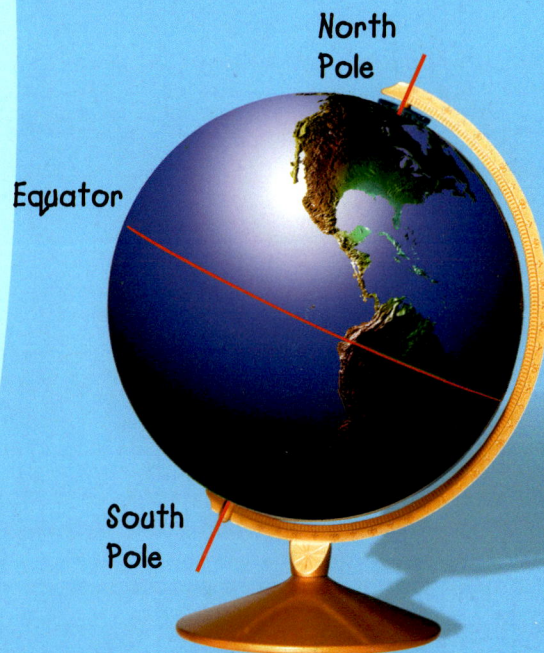

Chinese flag

EUROPE

ASIA

China

AFRICA

AUSTRALIA

ANTARCTICA

Emperor penguins live and breed on Antarctica.

North Pole

Equator

South Pole

The poles are the points to the extreme north and south of Earth. Because they curve away from the Sun, they are very cold. The North Pole lies in the frozen Arctic Ocean. The South Pole is on the icy continent of Antarctica.

Antarctica

What is this?

Page 23

All at sea

Most of the water on Earth is held in the oceans and seas. The area where land meets the sea is called the coast. The sea is powerful, with its moving tides and crashing waves. It slowly wears down the land, forming natural arches, cliffs and caves.

Page 30

5

6

The coast is a lively place. Lots of animals make their homes here, and many people like to live by the sea. Some people, such as fishermen, do their jobs out on the water. In this picture a fishing boat is bringing its catch back to harbour as the Sun rises in the morning.

Page 26

8

7

This is a close-up view of grains of sand. Sand is rock, broken down by waves.

Watery planet

Water can be found all over our planet. As well as in the sea there is water in lakes, rivers and ponds. Ice is frozen water and it covers large areas of land. Some water falls as rain, and some is underground.

Water vapour rises.

Water evaporates.

Rivers flow into the sea.

Arctic Ocean

Atlantic Ocean

Pacific Ocean

Pacific Ocean

Indian Ocean

Southern Ocean

Rivers are full of fresh water and flow across the land.

The River Seine runs through Paris, France.

Salty sea water fills the world's oceans. The three biggest oceans are the Atlantic Ocean, the Indian Ocean and the Pacific Ocean. The Pacific Ocean is the biggest of all.

People fish on Lake Victoria.

Lakes are large areas of water surrounded by land. Most lakes are full of fresh water. Lake Victoria in Africa is one of the biggest lakes in the world.

Clouds form.

Rain falls.

Some water sinks into the ground and is stored among soil and rock.

The water cycle is the movement of water around our planet. Heat from the Sun evaporates water from the surface of lakes and the sea, and it rises as water vapour. As it is pushed over high ground it turns into clouds and falls as rain. It then flows back down streams and rivers to the sea.

Rain can fall heavily sometimes!

A glacier flows down a mountain valley in Canada.

Glaciers are like rivers of ice. They flow very slowly downhill.

Ice covers the land in the world's coldest places. Many mountain peaks have caps of snow and ice, and ice flows down the valleys between them in glaciers. Ice also covers large areas of land near the poles.

These dogs are pulling a sled over ice near the North Pole.

Exploring the rainforest

Tropical rainforests are full of life. They are home to thousands of different kinds of plants and animals. Rainforest trees are some of the tallest on Earth. The biggest are over 60 metres high. Their branches are thickest at the top, forming what is known as the canopy.

Page 11

What is this?

1. boa constrictor
2. tarantula
3. scarlet macaw
4. fruit bat

This is a tree frog's foot. Tree frogs have sticky pads on their toes to help them grip branches.

At the end of the day, a group of scarlet macaws flies in to roost in a rainforest tree. Scarlet macaws are a type of parrot and they live in South America. All around them, other animals and birds fill the treetops. Some eat leaves or fruit, but others – like the boa constrictor – are hunters that eat other animals.

Page 14

Page 30

5 three-toed sloth   6 spider monkey   7 toucan   8 tree frog

Different biomes

A biome is a type of natural habitat – a place where particular kinds of plants and animals live. Tropical rainforest is a well-known biome, but there are many others too.

Deserts are very dry places where it is tough for life to survive. Even so, they have their own plants and animals. Snakes and lizards are particularly common here.

Giraffes roam on savannah lands.

This thorny devil can go for a long time without water.

Bushes grow among the dry grass.

Temperate grassland is found in cooler countries, outside the tropics. In many places it has been turned into farmland and it is now one of Earth's rarest biomes.

Prairie dogs live on temperate grassland in the USA.

Savannah is the name given to open grassland in Africa and other hot parts of the world. It is home to herds of grazing animals and the creatures that feed on them.

A brown bear claws a forest pine tree.

Coniferous forest is made up of trees such as pine and fir, which have needles instead of large leaves. It covers large areas of Canada, Scandinavia and Russia.

Most conifers have tall, straight trunks and downward-pointing branches.

Tundra is the biome nearest the poles. This is tundra in summer.

Tundra plants are small and low-growing.

Oceans and seas are home to more living things than any of the biomes on land. They are also the least explored parts of our planet. Less than 10 per cent of the ocean floor has been properly mapped, and much of the ocean is too deep for human divers to survive.

Coral reefs like this are found in shallow, tropical waters.

Yellow angelfish

Using the land

Imagine the world without any people. It would look very different! People have changed the landscape on Earth in many different ways. We have cut down trees, dug mines in the ground, made fields for farming and built homes and roads. Every day we change our planet a bit more.

Page 30

What is this?

2

1

① A plough digs up the soil.

② logs from a planted forest

③ quarry of stone for building

This is water flowing from a hydroelectric dam. Water turns turbines in the dam to make electricity.

This farmer is ploughing a field for crops to be planted. Crops and farm animals, like the cows in this valley, provide most of the food we eat. In the background we can see logging in a forest and diggers in a quarry. The wood and stone from these will be used for building.

Page 15

4. a town in the distance

5. hydroelectric dam

6. A reservoir stores water.

7. Wind turbines make electricity.

Earth and us

Every one of us has an impact on our planet. The homes we live in and the roads and railways we travel on have changed the natural landscape. People have removed forests and other habitats to create building space as well as farmland for our food.

Villages and towns are small built-up areas of houses and other buildings. Cities are larger and cover greater areas of land. Some of the biggest cities are home to millions of people.

Ports are coastal towns built for shipping.

This hillside village is in Italy.

Container ships carry goods between places.

People are destroying many of Earth's **natural habitats**. As rainforests are cut down for timber and farmland, the animals that lived in them are left without a home.

Orang-utans need forests.

Tokyo is the world's largest city and the capital of Japan.

Every country in the world has a **capital city**. This is usually where the government is based.

Trains provide us with high-speed travel.

These cooling towers are part of a coal-fired power station.

Pollution happens when we burn coal and other fossil fuels. Power stations, industry and motor vehicles all create polluting greenhouse gases. These contribute to global warming, which is melting ice at the poles and causing sea levels to rise.

Transport networks run between our villages, towns and cities so that we can get from place to place. Trains cross the land on railway lines. Cars and trucks use roads, which also cut through the landscape.

Solar panels and wind turbines make electricity without pollution.

Solar panels use energy from the Sun to create power.

flamingos, zebras and a wildebeest

Life

Earth is the only place in the Universe where we know life exists. Earth is home to millions of different **species** (types of living thing). The animals above are species from East Africa.

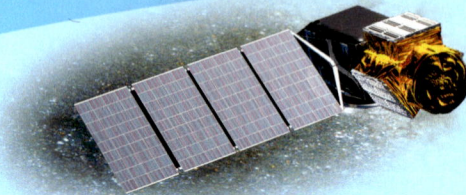

Rainforests are home to thousands of different living things. They all have their own place and way of life. Bats and many other creatures are **nocturnal** (active at night), and others are active in the daytime.

Science

This **satellite** is helping to map the Moon's surface. Other satellites are sent into orbit around Earth. They are used for everything from sending TV signals to forecasting the weather.

Building **dams** across rivers creates artificial lakes, called reservoirs. These provide our towns and cities with water. Turbines in the dams produce electricity.

Environment

Volcanic eruptions completely change the landscape. Ash covers the ground and can crush or bury houses. Lava burns whatever it touches, then cools to form solid rock.

Cliffs look solid but bits often break away as waves pound them. This process is called **erosion** and it can change the shape of a coastline over time.

arch

People

Java (in Indonesia) is the most densely populated island in the world and it is dotted with volcanoes. Many of its 130 million people are farmers, growing rice in the rich volcanic soil.

The first people to climb the world's tallest mountain, **Everest**, were Sir Edmund Hillary and Tenzing Norgay in 1953. The youngest person to climb it was 15-year-old Ming Kipa in 2003.

Hillary and Norgay

More to explore

Volcanic ash forms rich soil that is perfect for growing crops. All plants need minerals and other natural nutrients in order to grow. Soil near volcanoes is particularly rich in these minerals.

Coastal cliffs and islands may look bare and lifeless, but they provide nesting places for all sorts of **seabirds**. Here they are safe from ground-living hunters such as foxes, which might otherwise eat the chicks or eggs.

seagulls

As altitude (height above sea level) increases, the amount of **oxygen** in the air goes down. Most climbers wear breathing equipment in high mountains to make sure they have enough oxygen.

Rainforest plants have given us many different **medicines**. One reason for protecting rainforests is to protect their plants so that scientists can continue to study them.

Rainforests are important to the **environment** because they help to balance gases in the air. Plants take in carbon dioxide, a gas that can be harmful if there is too much of it. They give off oxygen, which all animals need to breathe.

rainforest plant

In **high mountain ranges**, temperatures are very cold. The water here is frozen. Glaciers are frozen rivers that change the landscape very slowly over time. The heavy ice grinds away at the ground and forms a U-shaped valley.

Fishing is an important industry for many coastal towns and villages. The people who work on fishing boats often work through the night and they may be away for days at a time.

Most **farmers** do particular jobs at certain times of the year. Ploughing takes place in autumn or early spring, depending on the type of crop to be planted.

Index